# An Analysis of the Impact of the Commercial Real Estate Concentration Guidance

**KEITH FRIEND**
Office of the Comptroller of the Currency

**HARRY GLENOS**
Office of the Comptroller of the Currency

**JOSEPH B. NICHOLS**
Federal Reserve Board of Governors

WASHINGTON, D.C. • APRIL 2013

# An Analysis of the Impact of the Commercial Real Estate Concentration Guidance

**KEITH FRIEND**
Office of the Comptroller of the Currency

**HARRY GLENOS**
Office of the Comptroller of the Currency

**JOSEPH B. NICHOLS**
Federal Reserve Board of Governors

WASHINGTON, D.C. • APRIL 2013

Keith Friend is a Research Analyst in the Economics Department of the Office of the Comptroller of the Currency. Harry Glenos is a Senior Financial Advisor in the Credit & Market Risk Policy Division of the Office of the Comptroller of the Currency. Joseph B. Nichols is an Economist with the Board of Governors of the Federal Reserve System. Please address correspondence to Joseph B. Nichols, Board of Governors of the Federal Reserve System, 20th and C Streets, NW, Washington, DC, 20551, Mail stop 1812, (202) 452-2983, joseph.b.nichols@frb.gov, or Harry Glenos, Office of the Comptroller of the Currency, 400 7th Street, SW, Washington, DC, 20219, (202) 649-6409, harry.glenos@occ.treas.gov. The authors wish to thank the communications units of our respective agencies for editorial assistance. The views expressed in this paper are those of the authors alone and do not necessarily reflect those of the Office of the Comptroller of the Currency or the Board of Governors of the Federal Reserve System. The authors take responsibility for any errors.

# Contents

# Part 1: Executive Summary

This paper analyzes aspects of the interagency guidance issued in 2006, titled "Concentrations in Commercial Real Estate Lending, Sound Risk Management Practices."[1] The recent financial crisis and recession provide an opportunity to consider the relationship between the guidance and banks' commercial real estate (CRE) concentrations and performance during the downturn. This paper also analyzes how the share of banking institutions with high levels of CRE concentration, as defined in the guidance, has changed over time (part 2); documents the effect of CRE concentrations on bank failures (part 3); and studies CRE loan growth and bank capital strength since the 2006 issuance of the guidance (part 4).[2]

The 2006 interagency guidance focuses on the risks of high levels of concentration in CRE lending at banking institutions, and specifically addresses two supervisory criteria:

- **Construction concentration criterion**: Loans for construction, land, and land development (CLD or "construction") represent 100 percent or more of a banking institution's total risk-based capital

- **Total CRE concentration criterion**: Total non-owner-occupied CRE loans (including CLD loans), as defined in the 2006 guidance ("total CRE"), represent 300 percent or more of the institution's total risk-based capital, **and** growth in total CRE lending has increased by 50 percent or more during the previous 36 months

The guidance states that banking institutions exceeding the concentration levels mentioned in the two supervisory criteria should have in place enhanced credit risk controls, including stress testing of CRE portfolios.[3] The guidance also states that institutions with CRE concentration levels above those specified in the two supervisory criteria may be identified for further supervisory analysis.

It should be noted that the supervisory criteria were not intended to establish hard limits or caps on banking institutions' CRE concentration levels. The 2006 guidance states that "numeric indicators do not constitute limits."[4] Therefore, banks with acceptable risk-management practices could retain their high CRE concentration levels. Additionally, the Total CRE criterion applied to institutions contains two joint conditions: (1) Total CRE above a certain level of capital **and** (2) rapid growth in Total CRE in the previous three years. Jointly applying both measures in the total CRE criterion significantly reduces the number of institutions exceeding it.

Our analysis found that 31 percent of all commercial banks in 2006 exceeded at least one of the concentration levels specified in the supervisory criteria. In 2006, these institutions held $378 billion in outstanding CRE loans, almost 40 percent of all outstanding CRE loans. Beginning in 2007, CRE exposures began to decline and, by the fourth quarter of 2011, the supervisory criteria for concentration levels applied to only 11 percent of institutions, which held $298 billion, or 34 percent, of all outstanding CRE loans. By and large, the institutions with CRE concentrations exceeding the concentration levels in 2011 also exceeded the levels in 2006. Since 2006, only a few banks have been "pushed over" the concentration levels by declining capital.

During the three-year economic downturn, banks with high CRE concentration levels proved to be far

[1] "Concentrations in Commercial Real Estate Lending, Sound Risk Management Practices," 71 *Federal Register* 238 (December 12, 2006), pp. 74580–74588 (www.occ.gov/news-issuances/federal-register/71fr74580.pdf).

[2] The paper excludes analysis of thrifts, both federal- and state-chartered. The Office of Thrift Supervision issued similar guidance under CEO Memo 252 (December 14, 2006), however, it did not contain the specific concentration limits contained in the interagency guidance for reasons described therein.

[3] The Congressional Oversight Panel documented the public debate about the guidance's issuance in its February 2010, report "Commercial Real Estate Losses and the Risk to Financial Stability" (www.gpo.gov/fdsys/pkg/CPRT-111JPRT54785/pdf/CPRT-111JPRT54785.pdf) as part of the panel's oversight of the Emergency Economic Stabilization Act of 2008.

[4] 71 *Federal Register* 238 (December 12, 2006) pp. 74584, paragraph 3.

more susceptible to failure. Using call report data and applying the supervisory criteria for concentration levels, this paper identifies several findings about the effect of CRE lending on bank performance during the recent market downturn. These findings include:

- Among banks that exceeded both supervisory criteria, 23 percent failed during the three-year economic downturn, compared with 0.5 percent of banks for which neither of the criteria was exceeded. In particular, 13 percent of banks that exceeded the Construction criterion failed. Banks exceeding the Construction criterion alone accounted for an estimated 80 percent of the losses to the Federal Deposit Insurance Corporation insurance fund from 2007 to 2011.

- Banks that exceeded the supervisory criteria on CRE concentration levels were more likely than banks that did not exceed the criteria to shrink the size of their CRE portfolios from 2008 to 2011, primarily by reducing their holdings of Construction loans.

- A non-trivial number of banks exceeding the supervisory criteria on concentration levels in 2007 continued to increase their CRE concentrations through 2011. This was consistent with the guidance's absence of hard caps on CRE concentrations.

- Banks that exceeded the supervisory criteria on CRE concentrations tended to experience greater deterioration in condition as assessed by market participants. Our analysis reveals that banks with higher CRE concentrations experienced larger declines in their market capital ratio (MCR) during the recent economic downturn.

# Part 2: Changes in CRE Concentrations over Time

In December 2006, the Board of Governors of the Federal Reserve System, the Federal Deposit Insurance Corporation (FDIC), and the Office of the Comptroller of the Currency (OCC) (collectively, "the agencies") issued interagency guidance, titled "Concentrations in Commercial Real Estate Lending, Sound Risk Management Practices" ("the guidance"). The purpose of the guidance is to address banking institutions' increased concentrations of CRE loans relative to their capital. The guidance reminds institutions that strong risk-management practices and appropriate levels of capital are important elements of sound CRE lending programs, particularly when institutions have concentrations in CRE loans.

As CRE loans begin to account for larger shares of bank loans, the concern is that banks with elevated levels of CRE concentration need to have appropriate risk-management practices in place for the level of exposure in their CRE portfolios. The guidance is meant to reinforce and enhance the agencies' existing regulations and guidelines for real estate lending and loan portfolio management.

The guidance does not establish specific CRE lending limits or caps; rather, it states that an institution exceeding concentration levels may be identified for further supervisory analysis, focusing on the level and nature of the institution's CRE concentration risk. Specifically, the guidance identifies two supervisory criteria that could subject an institution to further analysis:

* **Construction concentration criterion**: An institution's CLD loan concentration levels represent 100 percent or more of its total risk-based capital (the CLD ratio)

* **Total CRE concentration criterion**: An institution's total non-owner-occupied CRE loans (including CLD loans), as defined in the guidance, represent 300 percent or more of its total risk-based capital

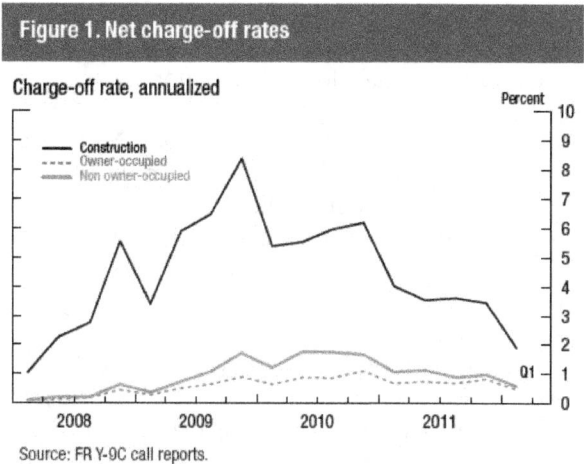

**Figure 1. Net charge-off rates**

Charge-off rate, annualized

— Construction
--- Owner-occupied
--- Non owner-occupied

Source: FR Y-9C call reports.

(the total ratio), **and** its non-owner-occupied CRE loans have increased by 50 percent or more during the previous 36 months (the growth component).[5]

The construction concentration criterion focuses exclusively on CLD loans, as those loans are the most likely to result in losses during a downturn. CLD lending is naturally highly cyclical. Building demand tends to rise quickly when credit availability is high and underwriting discipline relaxes, then contracts sharply during downturns. Figure 1 compares banks' net charge-off rates for construction loans, owner-occupied CRE loans, and non-owner-occupied CRE loans. Clearly, construction loans have had much higher loss rates during the recent market downturn. Loss rates for non-owner-occupied loans, while still

---

[5] Owner-occupied CRE loans were not broken out by financial institutions in call report data until 2007; therefore, it was not possible to accurately measure the three-year growth rate of an institution's non-owner-occupied CRE portfolio—and correctly apply the growth component—until late 2010. Given this data limitation, we use a measure of the second criteria without this condition applied in the historical analysis in this paper; however, it is important to recognize the growth component as laid out in the guidance. The appendix provides details on ratio calculations using call report definitions.

higher than loss rates for owner-occupied loans, were significantly lower than those for construction loans.

The guidance does not state that the supervisory criteria should be viewed as a hard cap on CRE concentration levels. Institutions are permitted to maintain CRE concentration levels above the levels as defined in the supervisory criteria, as long as the institutions can document heightened risk-management practices related to their CRE portfolios. These heightened risk-management practices may include stress tests, although the sophistication level of the stress tests should be appropriate for the institution's size.

The guidance's goal is not to discourage banks from responding to demand for credit. Rather, the goal is to address concerns that banks entering the CRE market and rapidly increasing their CRE concentration levels might not have the institutional knowledge, well-developed and documented risk-management practices, or capital necessary to address the increase in CRE risk exposures. CRE concentration levels at banks have steadily increased in the past two decades, increasing banks' exposures to the unique risks associated with CRE lending. The recession period reveals again the cyclical nature of the CRE market. Excessive CRE concentrations pose a threat even to banks with good risk practices and above-average capital, particularly in the most overheated markets that were the hardest to fall. The recession also revealed that, while good risk-management practices and above-average capital are essential to mitigate risks associated with high CRE concentrations, they may not be sufficient to prevent bank failure.

## Applying the Interagency Guidance

In figure 2, we use bank-level call report data to illustrate how banks' CRE concentration levels have changed since 2008 relative to the supervisory criteria.[6] The two bar charts in the top panel of figure 2 illustrate how applying either of the two criteria affects

- the percentage of banks close to or exceeding the concentration levels and

- the amount of outstanding CRE loans held by banks when sorted by concentration levels of CRE lending

---

[6] The appendix to this report provides instructions for correctly calculating the supervisory criteria using the post-2007 call report definitions.

The middle and bottom panels of figure 2 apply the criteria separately—by construction concentrations and by total CRE concentrations, respectively. For both the construction and total ratios, the sample of banks is divided into three categories: (1) banks are considered *concentrated* if their ratios are above the concentration levels (300 percent or 100 percent, respectively); (2) banks are considered *nearly concentrated* if their ratios are close to the concentration levels (between 250 and 300 percent or between 80 and 100 percent, respectively); and (3) banks are considered *unconcentrated* if their ratios are not close to the levels set in the guidance (less than 250 percent or less than 80 percent, respectively).

In figure 2, the pair of charts in the top panel shows the effect of having either ratio binding. As shown in the top chart at left, almost 40 percent of all commercial banks in 2008 had at least one of the ratios close to or above the thresholds. By the fourth quarter of 2011, this number had fallen to less than 20 percent. As shown in the top chart at right, banks above at least one of the thresholds held $378 billion in, or 40 percent of, outstanding CRE loans in 2008, and $298 billion, or 34 percent, in 2011.

While there has been a significant reduction in the number of banks close to or above at least one of the thresholds, banks that remain close to or exceeding the thresholds still account for nearly half of all outstanding CRE loans. We believe this indicates that there is a core group of banks that specializes in, or is particularly dependent on, CRE lending. Many banks with high concentrations that managed to survive the recession benefitted from being outside the most overheated and affected markets. This likely was not the case for all surviving banks, which suggests that at least some of them were able to effectively manage the risks of holding concentrated CRE portfolios, including by employing risk management practices that satisfy the demands of the guidance.

The pair of charts in the middle panel of figure 2 repeats this analysis based solely on the construction ratio. The definitions of concentrated, nearly concentrated, and unconcentrated here depend only on the ratio of CLD loans to total capital. The chart at left shows that the share of banks with ratios above or near 100 percent declined from 35 percent in 2008 to 11 percent in 2011. The chart at right illustrates sharp declines in both the total amount of CLD loans outstanding (from $392 billion in 2008 to $207 billion in 2011) and the share of those loans held by banks near or above the construction ratio (from 55 percent

## Figure 2. Change in banks' CRE concentrations since 2008 relative to the guidance

### Impact of Either Ratio Binding

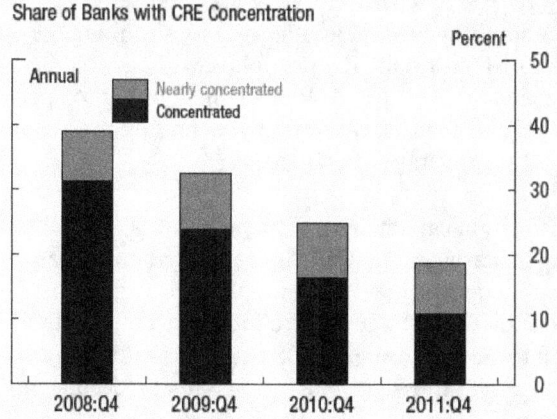

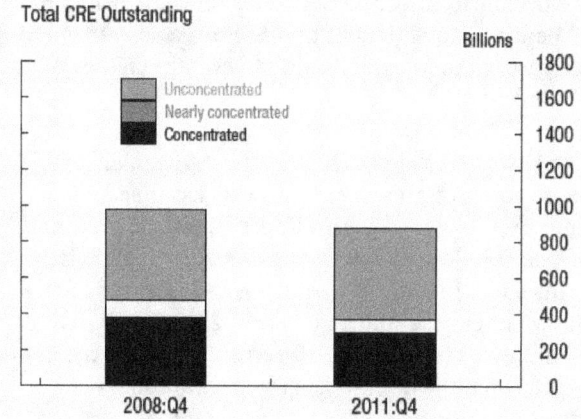

### Impact of Construction Ratio Binding

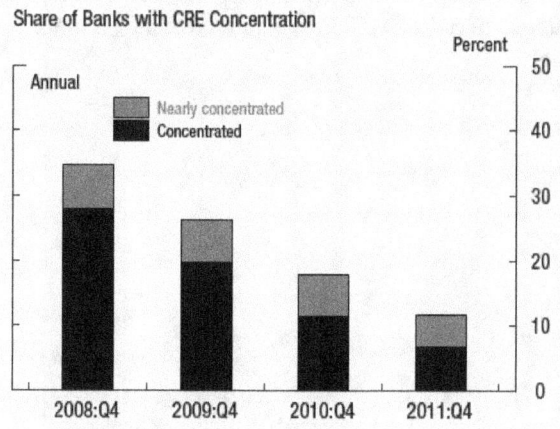

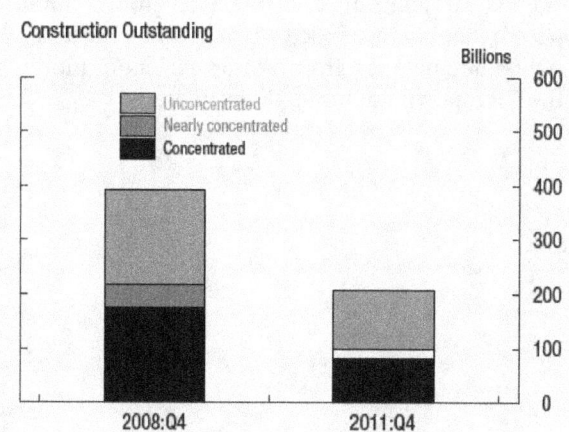

### Impact of Total Ratio Binding

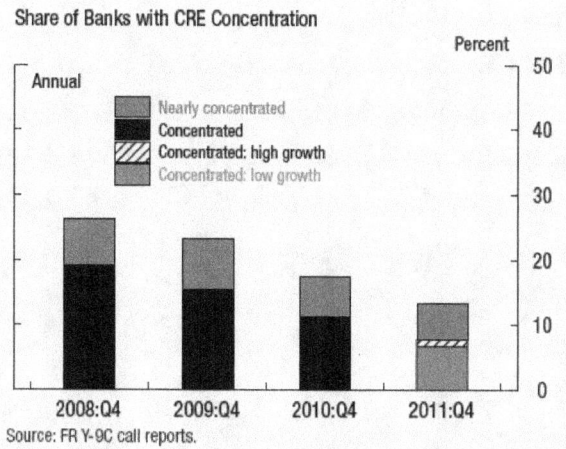

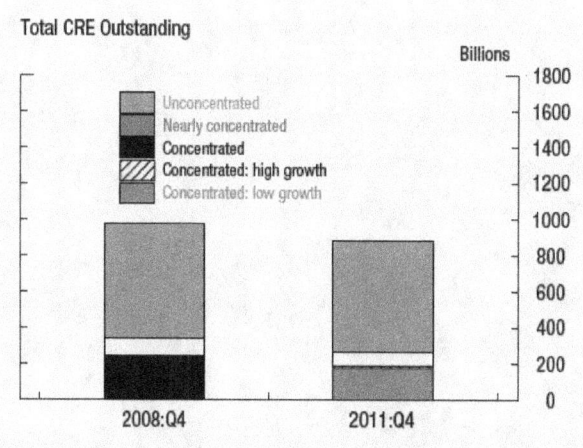

Source: FR Y-9C call reports.

to 47 percent). Almost all of the banks (97 percent) that saw their ratios fall from above 100 percent in 2008 to below 100 percent in 2011 did so at least in part by contracting their CLD portfolios. The average decline in the CLD portfolios for these banks was 51 percent. Roughly half of these banks also saw increases in their capital, with an average change of 22 percent.

The bottom panel of figure 2 repeats the analysis based solely on the total non-owner-occupied CRE ratio. As shown in the two upper panels, 27 percent of banks holding 35 percent of outstanding CRE loans had a total ratio close to or above the concentration level set in the guidance in 2008, compared with only 14 percent and 30 percent, respectively, in 2011. When the additional growth component—growth of 50 percent or more in CRE loans over the previous 36 months—is applied to the 2011 data, however, the criteria are applicable for less than 2 percent of banks, which hold 2 percent of the outstanding CRE loans in 2011. When the growth component is incorrectly applied—by excluding the additional requirement for growth of 50 percent or more in the CRE portfolio during the previous

36 months—a significant number of additional institutions are misidentified as subject to the guidance. As we observed with the construction ratio, most of the banks (91 percent) that saw their ratios fall from more than 300 percent to less than 300 percent accomplished this at least in part by shrinking the size of their total CRE portfolios, with an average decline of 24 percent. Many of these banks (45 percent) also reduced this ratio by increasing their capital, by an average of 30 percent.

Growth in capital and contraction in CRE portfolios, particularly among CLD loans, contributed to an overall decline in CRE concentrations over the period. The average construction concentration ratio fell from 77 percent in 2008 to 38 percent in 2011. The total ratio saw a much less dramatic decline, from 177 percent to 141 percent, over the same period. Much of the decline in the total ratio is due to shrinking CLD portfolios. Despite these declines in concentration, a significant number of banks remain heavily concentrated in CRE loans, and exposure to non-CLD CRE loans in particular remains high.

# Part 3: The Impact of CRE Concentrations on Bank Failures

One of the concerns that spurred issuance of the guidance was that institutions with high CRE concentration levels that lack the strong risk-management practices required by the guidance are more vulnerable during economic downturns and more likely to fail. To test the validity of this concern, we analyzed the 7,379 active commercial bank charters from March 31, 2007, to September 30, 2011, to determine whether institutions exceeding the supervisory criteria concentration levels defined in the guidance actually were more likely to fail.[7] We took a snapshot of banks on March 31, 2007, and performed our analysis using the concentration levels specified in the supervisory criteria.

We categorized each bank according to whether or not it exceeded the supervisory criteria concentration levels, its Tier 1 capital ratio, and other characteristics on March 31, 2007. We tracked the banks through September 30, 2011, without regard to any actions taken in the interim. Figure 3 summarizes our findings.

There is a major difference in the failure rates for banks above and below the concentration levels specified in the supervisory criteria. Of the banks that met or exceeded both concentration levels and the growth component in the supervisory criteria, 22.9 percent failed. In contrast, only 0.5 percent of banks that had concentration levels lower than those in the supervisory criteria failed.

We extended our analysis to include other factors that might contribute to higher failure rates. These

---

[7] The three-month period ending March 31, 2007, is the first quarter for which call reports included details adequate to test the guidance criteria. Before that date, owner-occupied and non-owner-occupied commercial mortgages were not reported separately.

---

**Figure 3. Bank failure rates by supervisory criteria**

Our analysis tracks 7,379 active national and state-chartered banks between March 31, 2007, and September 30, 2011, and calculates rates of failure relative to supervisory criteria on CRE concentration levels

| Supervisory criteria | Number of banks[1] | Failure rate (percent) |
|---|---|---|
| Does not meet or exceed either supervisory criteria | 3,755 | 0.5 |
| Meets or exceeds both supervisory criteria | 772 | 22.9 |
| CLD is 100 percent or more of total risk-based capital[2] | 1,909 | 13.0 |
| Total CRE is 300 percent or more of capital and CRE portfolio meets growth component in second supervisory criteria | 890 | 20.6 |
| Total CRE is 300 percent or more | 1,310 | 16.3 |
| Total CRE 36-month growth rate is 50 percent or more | 2,819 | 9.9 |
| Total CRE is 300 percent or more of capital and 36-month growth rate is 50 percent or more, but CLD is below 100 percent | 118 | 5.1 |
| CRE portfolio meets 36-month period growth criteria, but CLD is below 100 percent and total CRE is below 300 percent | 1,496 | 4.8 |

Note: Ratio values used were a snapshot as of March 31, 2007. Excludes owner-occupied, non-farm, non-residential CRE. Growth was determined using total CRE on a call report basis since owner-occupied could not be eliminated, lacking data prior to 2007.

[1] Components do not add to total because of overlapping criteria, bank mergers, or other eliminations.

[2] Banks meeting or exceeding the CLD concentration levels are estimated to have resulted in 80 percent of losses to the FDIC insurance fund between 2007 and 2011. Banks in this category that did survive to September 30, 2011, mostly have CAMELS ratings of 3, 4, or 5, based on national bank data.

Source: OCC, Federal Financial Institutions Examination Council (FFIEC) call report data.

factors include banks with a low Tier 1 capital ratio, a high dependency on brokered deposits, and proximity to markets experiencing the most intense downturns. None of these factors had as strong an impact in determining risk of failure as CLD concentration levels.

Most bank failures were seen in banks that had CLD concentration levels greater than 100 percent of capital. Some 13 percent of the 1,909 banks (charters) with CLD-to-total risk-based capital ratios higher than 100 percent failed. Roughly 60 percent of the survivors in the same category with high CLD concentration levels as of September 30, 2011, were in poor condition, receiving CAMELS ratings of 3, 4, or 5.[8] Using FDIC data, we estimate that 80 percent of total FDIC insurance fund costs from this period are associated with banks whose CLD lending was 100 percent or more of total risk-based capital.[9] The nature of CLD lending is that risks are higher than for other types of CRE lending; historically, net charge-off rates for CLD lending have been much higher than for commercial mortgage finance.

About 21 percent of the 890 banks exceeding the concentration levels in the total CRE concentration criterion, which incorporates both CLD and non-owner-occupied commercial mortgage CRE concentration and the 50 percent growth in CRE portfolio component, failed. If the CRE growth component is disregarded, the failure rate for this group of banks falls to 16.3 percent. The total CRE supervisory criterion, however, overlaps with the first criterion on CLD concentration levels, because CLD loans are also included in the non-owner-occupied CRE ratio

calculation. When restricting the sample to banks that exceeded the total CRE concentration level—but remained below the 100 percent CLD concentration level—and had less than 50 percent CRE growth during the previous 36 months, 4.6 percent failed. While this failure rate is higher than that of banks that met or exceeded none of the criteria (0.5 percent), it is considerably lower than the failure rate among banks that exceeded the supervisory criteria on CLD concentration levels.

Banks with total CRE growth greater than 50 percent, ignoring for the moment other components of the supervisory criteria, saw a failure rate of 9.9 percent. Restricting this sample further, to just those banks whose concentration levels are below those specified in the supervisory criteria, the failure rate falls to 4.8 percent. While this failure rate is higher than that of banks that met none of the criteria (0.5 percent), it is also considerably lower than the failure rate among banks that exceeded the CLD concentration levels. Nevertheless, rapid portfolio growth is a longstanding warning signal that a bank's risk management and underwriting standards may be failing to recognize a build-up of risk within the bank.

Our analysis emphasizes the effect of CRE concentrations—in particular, concentrations in CLD loans—on the probability of bank failure. Figure 4 provides detailed results of our analysis of the relationship between CRE concentration levels and bank failure.

In figure 4, the top bar chart shows failure rates by the ratio of CLD loans to capital. The failure rate is about 2 percent when CLD concentration levels are below 100 percent of total risk-based capital. For banks in a range of 100 to 200 percent CLD exposure, the failure rate rises to 6 percent. The failure rate rises even more sharply—to 46 percent—for banks whose CLD concentration levels are more than 400 percent of total risk-based capital.

This trend shows that supervisory expectations for higher capital may play a crucial role. As banks increase their CLD concentration levels to more than 100 percent but less than 200 percent of total capital, banks with Tier 1 capital ratios exceeding critical levels experienced lower failure rates.[10] When CLD con-

---

[8]    CAMELS (Capital, Assets, Management, Earnings, Liquidity, and Sensitivity) is a rating system employed by banking regulators to assess the soundness of commercial banks. Ratings of 3, 4, or 5 may subject banks to enforcement actions, enhanced monitoring, and limitations on expansion. CAMELS ratings were available only for a sample subset of national banks; state charter CAMELS were not available for this analysis.

[9]    A list of failed banks and assisted transactions is available on www.FDIC.gov. As of November 15, 2011, and covering the period dating from March 31, 2007, 352 failed banking institutions (excluding savings charters) were identified by certificate number. Of these, the FDIC published loss estimates on 272 (up to December 31, 2010) at the time of the research. Loss estimates ranged from 3 to 61 percent of the banks' total assets. For the 272 banks, approximately 80 percent of the total estimated losses were for banks exceeding the 100 percent CLD concentration level. The mean loss percentage of total assets was 29.0 percent, and the median loss percentage of the 272 banks was 27.9 percent of total assets. The median of 27.9 percent was applied as an estimate for the 80 banks for which the FDIC provided no loss estimate. For the 352 failed banks as estimated, approximately 80 percent of the estimated total losses were in banks exceeding the 100 percent CLD concentration level.

[10]    Staff analysis not reported in this paper found that the critical level for the Tier 1 capital ratio for this subset of institutions was 11 percent. Additional analysis is available from the authors upon request.

**Figure 4. Failure rate by construction and land development exposure to capital and failure rate by total CRE exposure to capital**

Fail Rate by Construction and Land Development Exposure to Capital

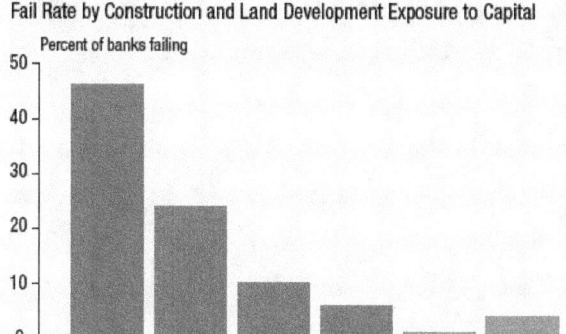

Fail Rate by Total CRE Exposure to Capital

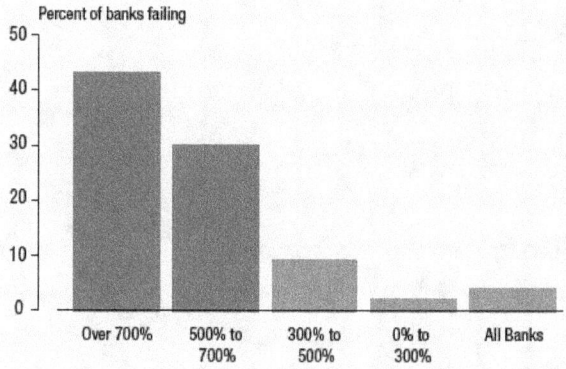

Source: OCC staff analysis.

centration levels rose beyond 200 percent of capital, elevated levels of capital reduced failures but did not prevent failure rates from rising sharply.

The bottom bar chart in figure 4 presents a similar analysis using the ratio of non-owner-occupied CRE loans to capital. The failure rates increase as total CRE concentrations rise, but not as drastically when CLD-only concentrations increase. In addition, the inclusion of CLD loans in the non-owner-occupied CRE criteria results in increased CLD concentrations also contributing to overall CRE concentrations. This finding is consistent with the net charge-off rates presented in figure 1, showing significantly higher loss rates among CLD loans.

# Part 4: Impact of the Guidance and Market Conditions on CRE Loan Growth

This chapter highlights the relationship between CRE concentrations and the growth of CRE loans at banks. There are three important notes about our analysis.

- Because of data limitations, we were unable to apply a component of the total CRE concentration criterion, regarding the 36-month growth of 50 percent or more in the non-owner-occupied CRE portfolio, to the historical data. As a result, the analyses for this chapter uses total CRE loans (including CLD loans) representing 300 percent or more of the institution's total risk-based capital.

- Second, while we did not perform a formal econometric test to determine whether or not we would have seen the same degree of change in CRE loan growth if the guidance had not been issued, a simple comparison is illustrative that banks with higher CRE concentrations retreated from CRE lending in response to market conditions more rapidly than lower concentration banks.

- Third, it is likely that geographically many of the banks with excessive CRE concentrations were in markets that experienced the sharpest corrections. From a policy or guidance perspective, we would expect geographic variation in the intensity of a market upturn or downturn to amplify bank risk-management efforts as well as supervisory concerns about the risks of the concentration of credit.

Figure 5 presents estimates of the distribution of the growth rates of CRE concentration levels from 2008 to 2011. We compute the average quarterly percent changes for that period. We use a merger-adjusted database of call report data to ensure that we are comparing growth rates for banks active throughout our analysis' time frame. For each chart in figure 5, we present an estimate of the distribution of the growth rates, using the same categories as defined in figure 2.

The top panel of charts in figure 5 reports the growth distributions based on whether either of the two components of the total CRE supervisory criterion is met. The chart at left shows the growth distributions for CLD loans, while the chart at right shows the growth distribution for non-owner-occupied, non-CLD CRE loans. While a significant majority of all banks saw declines in their holdings of CLD loans, banks above or near at least one of the concentration levels saw significantly greater declines. There is less of a difference in the distribution of the growth in non-CLD CRE loans, with many banks, even those defined as concentrated, seeing increases in non-CLD CRE loans.

The middle panel of charts in figure 5 repeats this analysis based only on whether the CLD criteria were applicable. Again, there is a sharp decline in CLD loans at the concentrated and nearly concentrated banks, and less of a difference in the growth rate of non-CLD loans between banks with different degrees of concentration in CLD loans.

The bottom panel of charts repeats the analysis based only on whether the total ratio supervisory criteria were met. The charts show that banks close to or above the supervisory criteria for the total ratio were more likely to show greater contractions in their holding of both CLD and non-CLD CRE loans. The gap in the change in loan growth between concentrated and unconcentrated banks, however, is greater for CLD loans than for non-CLD CRE loans.

**Figure 5. Estimates of distribution of growth rates in CRE concentration levels from 2008 to 2011**

## Impact of Either Ratio Binding

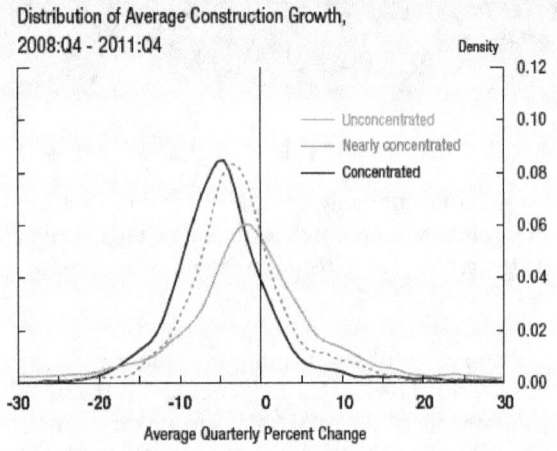

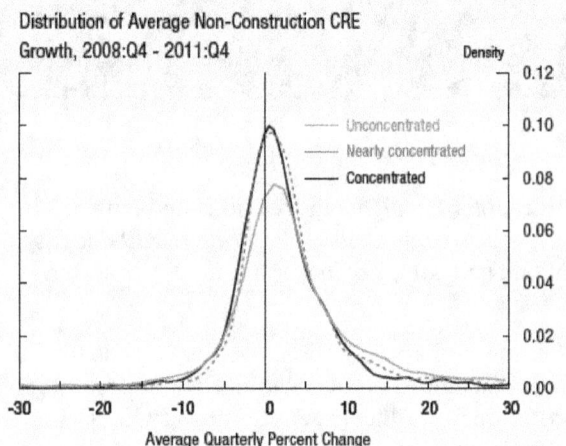

## Impact of Construction Ratio Binding

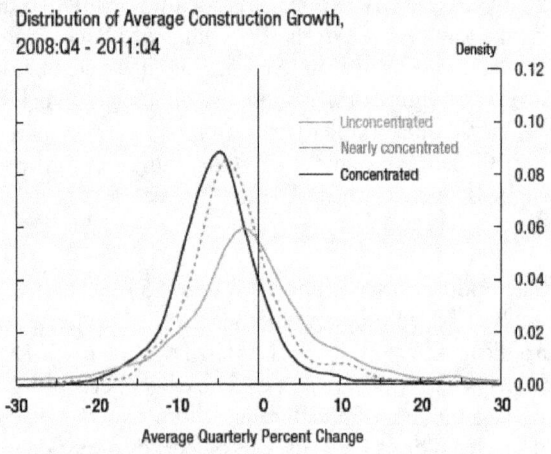

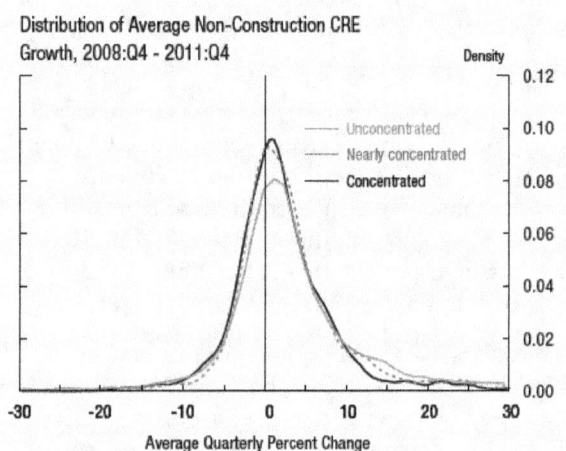

## Impact of Total Ratio Binding

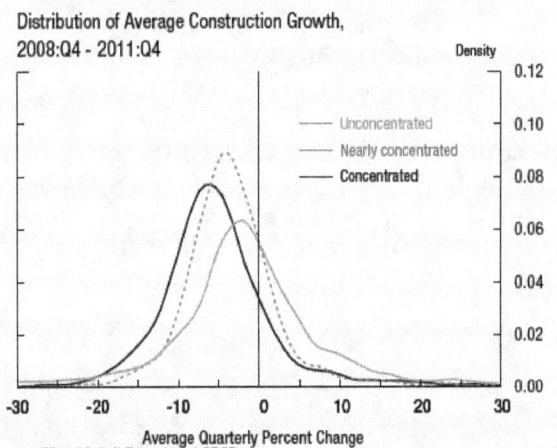

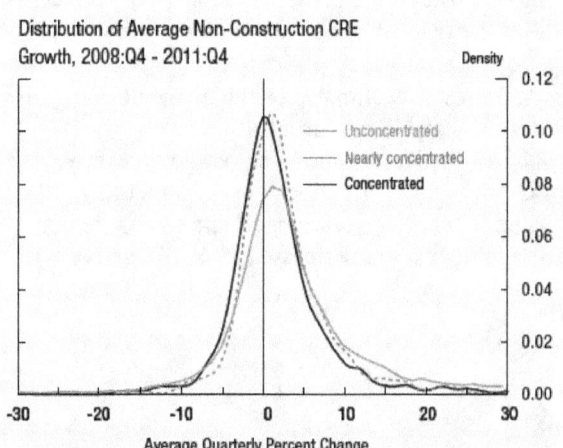

Source: FR Y-9C Call Report and CRSP.

Note: Bank holding companies are assigned to both a CLD and total CRE cohort based on their loan concentrations as of 2006:Q4. Subsequent measurements of the cohort's average MCR are based on all the BHCs that have survived to date. Total CRE includes loans secured by non-farm, non-residential properties (owner-occupied loans were not separately distinguished within these loans until 2008:Q1).

# Part 5: Impact of CRE Concentrations on Banks' Market Capital Ratio

In this chapter, our analysis looks at the effect of CRE concentrations on banks' capital strength as revealed by equity market data. Option pricing theory provides a method for computing a market-based measure of a bank holding company's (BHC) capital position.[11] This measure, referred to here as the market capital ratio (MCR), incorporates market knowledge of both the individual bank and of macroeconomic conditions to adjust the book value of assets. (Often, the book value includes components that are carried at cost and do not reflect economic reality.) Because it is based on market information, the MCR may be more forward-looking than more traditional capital measures that are based on reported financial data.

Our analysis looks at data for 325 publicly traded BHCs from the fourth quarter of 2006 through the first quarter of 2009. Reported book values come from the BHC's FR Y-9C call reporting forms, while the stock market data are sourced from the Center for Research in Security Prices (CRSP).[12] Only BHCs that were both publicly traded and whose stock data could be identified in CRSP are included in the sample.

Reported loan amounts for CLD as well as total CRE are used in combination with the amount of total risk-based capital to classify each BHC as either over or under one of the concentration levels speci-

fied in the supervisory criteria. This initial classification is based on each BHC's status as of the fourth quarter of 2006. Then, each BHC is assigned to a particular cohort whose performance is tracked over time. The cohorts are defined based on various combinations of the supervisory criteria. Figure 6 reports some of the summary results of this analysis.

The top panel in figure 6 reports the average MCR for BHCs that did not exceed either of the supervisory criteria concentration levels and for BHCs that did exceed at least one of the levels. Clearly, BHCs that exceeded both concentration levels began with lower MCRs at the time the guidance was issued and saw greater declines in their MCRs over time.

The middle and bottom panels in figure 6 repeat the analysis separately for each component and show consistent results.

Figures 7 through 12 illustrate changes over time in each cohort's MCR. The change in MCR is measured as the BHC's raw percentage decline between the fourth quarter of 2006 and the first quarter of 2009. The average decline is then calculated for each cohort, and confidence bounds are constructed using t statistics. The final row in each table uses a t-test to compare the difference in the declines of the two cohorts.

The group of BHCs whose CLD concentration was below 100 percent of total risk-based capital experienced a capital decline that was 3.6 percentage points less than those whose concentration exceeded 100 percent, as shown in figure 7. The BHCs below the total CRE concentration level of the supervisory criteria also saw a statistically smaller average decline in MCR than the average of those above the level, as shown in figure 8.

We next look at the effect of the total CRE supervisory criterion, which includes the growth component. When the growth component is used in conjunction with the total CRE concentration levels specified in

---

[11] The MCR is equal to one minus the ratio of book debt to market implied value of assets. The market implied asset value is determined by assuming the bank's equity is a call option on assets (the Merton model). Stock market data provide measures of the value of equity and equity volatility. For a discussion of methods and the underlying theory, see M. Gizycki and M. Levonian, "A Decade of Australian Banking Risk: Evidence from Share Prices." *RBA Research Discussion Papers*. Reserve Bank of Australia, 1993 (http://econpapers.repec.org/RePEc:rba:rbardp:rdp9302).

[12] The FR Y-9C reporting form collects basic financial data from a domestic BHC on a consolidated basis in the form of a balance sheet, an income statement, and detailed supporting schedules, including a schedule of off-balance-sheet items. CRSP is a non-profit research center at the Booth School of Business of the University of Chicago that provides historical stock market data.

**Figure 6. Change in Market Capital Ratio**

### Impact of Either Ratio Binding

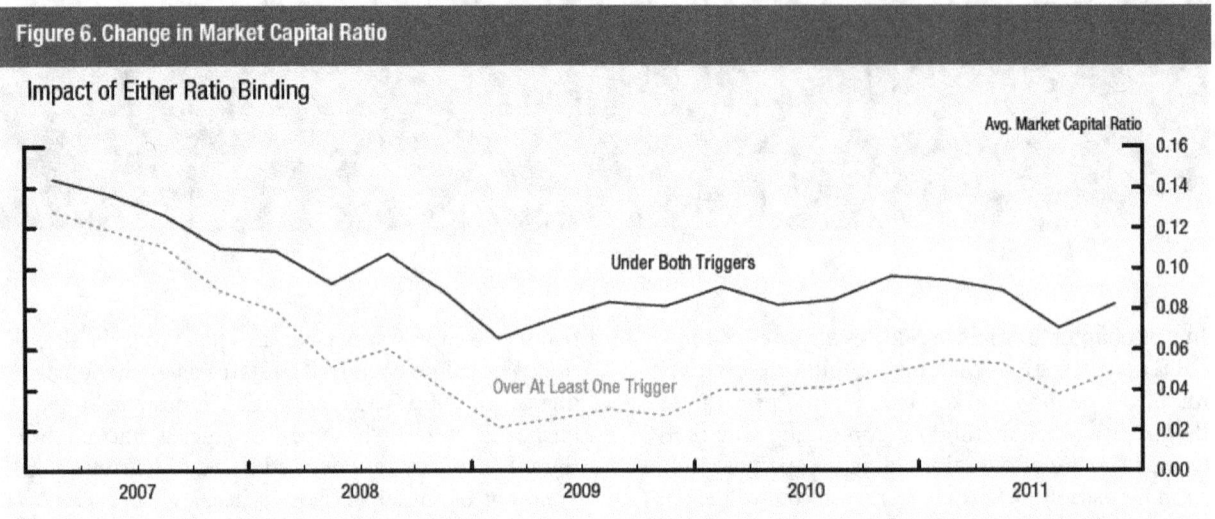

### Impact of Construction Ratio Binding

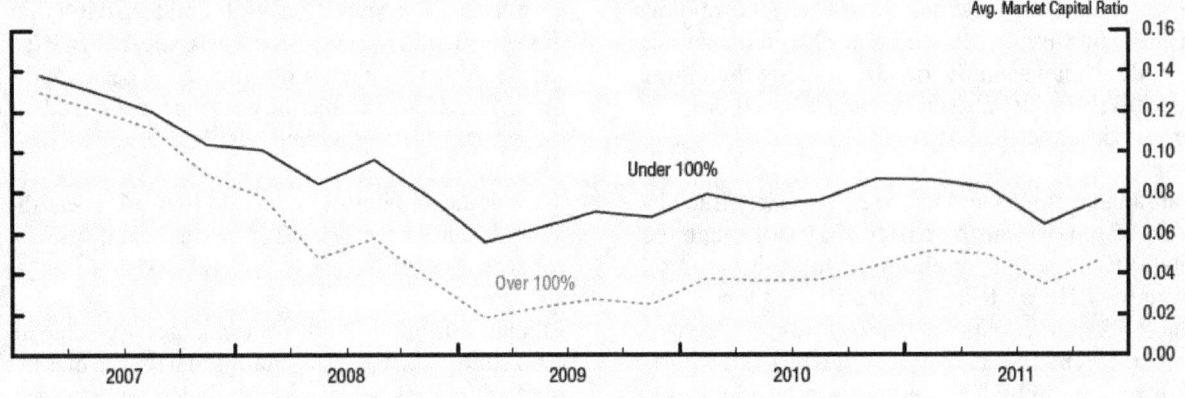

### Impact of Total Ratio Binding

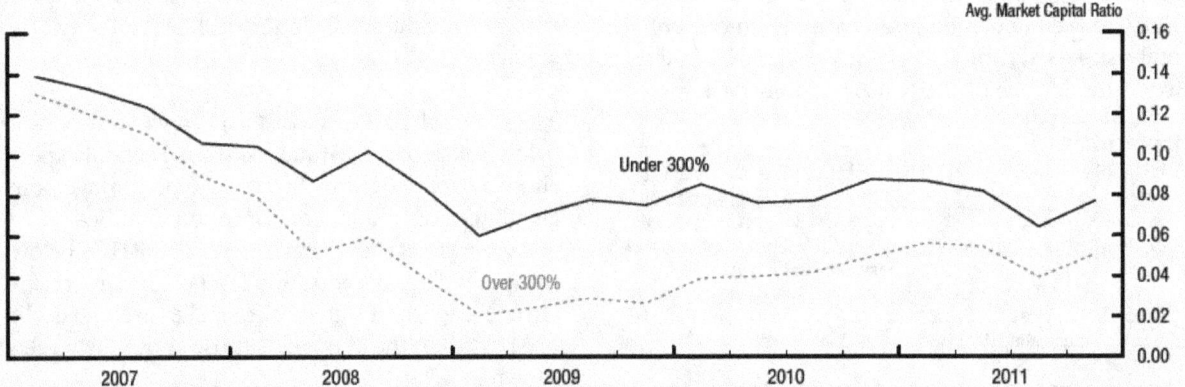

Source: Y-9C call reports and CRSP.

Note: Bank holding companies are assigned to both a CLD and total CRE cohort based on their loan concentrations as of 2006:Q4. Subsequent measurements of the cohort's average MCR are based on all the BHCs that have survived to date. Total CRE includes secured by non-farm, non-residential properties (owner-occupied loans were not separately distinguished within these loans until 2008:Q1).

the supervisory criteria, fewer banks are classified as exceeding the concentration level. Of the 325 BHCs, the data necessary to calculate the three-year growth rate were available for only 275, and only 36 of those BHCs had CRE representing more than 300 percent of total risk-based capital and more than 50 percent growth in their CRE concentration levels over the previous 36 months. The average decline in the MCR for these 36 BHCs was not significantly different from the average decline of the other 239 BHCs, as shown in figure 9.

Combining the classifications from figures 7 and 9 to create an overall guidance grouping shows that the BHCs that did not meet or exceed either of the supervisory criteria had a significantly smaller decline in capital than those that met or exceeded at least one. This grouping follows the same logic as the guidance itself. The estimated additional decline in

the MCR for the group of banks that met or exceeded at least one of the supervisory criteria was 4.0 percentage points greater than the MCR decline for those that did not, as shown in figure 10.

Finally, figures 11 and 12 illustrate the marginal effect of the total CRE component of the supervisory criteria with and without the growth component. When the growth component is ignored, BHCs with CLD concentration levels below 100 percent, but total CRE concentration levels above 300 percent, show a significantly larger decline in MCR than BHCs that are under both concentration levels. When the growth component is incorporated, however, that

### Figure 7. Construction

| C&D cohort | Number of BHCs | Average change in MCR (percent) | 95 percent confidence bounds (percent) | |
|---|---|---|---|---|
| | | | Lower | Upper |
| Over 100 percent | 160 | -12.5 | -13.3 | -11.8 |
| Under 100 percent | 165 | -8.9 | -9.7 | -8.2 |
| Difference | | -3.6 | -4.7 | -2.6 |

Source: Y-9C call reports and CRSP.

### Figure 8. Total CRE only

| Total CRE cohort | Number of BHCs | Average change in MCR (percent) | 95 percent confidence bounds (percent) | |
|---|---|---|---|---|
| | | | Lower | Upper |
| Over 300 percent | 188 | -12.3 | -13.0 | -11.5 |
| Under 300 percent | 137 | -8.6 | -9.3 | -7.8 |
| Difference | | -3.7 | -4.8 | -2.7 |

Source: Y-9C call reports and CRSP.

### Figure 9. Total CRE with growth component

| Total CRE cohort | Number of BHCs | Average change in MCR (percent) | 95 percent confidence bounds (percent) | |
|---|---|---|---|---|
| | | | Lower | Upper |
| Over 300 percent and > 50 percent growth | 36 | -11.5 | -12.7 | -10.4 |
| Under 300 percent or < 50 percent growth | 239 | -10.3 | -11.0 | -9.7 |
| Difference | | -1.2 | -3.0 | 0.6 |

Source: Y-9C call reports and CRSP.

### Figure 10. Dual guidance category

| Guidance group | Number of BHCs | Average change in MCR (percent) | 95 percent confidence bounds (percent) | |
|---|---|---|---|---|
| | | | Lower | Upper |
| Above at least one threshold | 166 | -12.5 | -13.2 | -11.8 |
| Below both thresholds | 140 | -8.6 | -9.3 | -7.8 |
| Difference | | -4.0 | -5.0 | -2.9 |

Note: Based on total CRE growth provision.
Source: Y-9C call reports and CRSP.

### Figure 11. Total CRE conditioned on construction

| C&D cohort | CRE cohort | Number of BHCs | Average change in MCR (percent) | 95 percent confidence bounds (percent) | |
|---|---|---|---|---|---|
| | | | | Lower | Upper |
| Under 100 percent | Over 300 percent | 49 | -10.4 | -12.0 | -8.8 |
| Under 100 percent | Under 300 percent | 116 | -8.3 | -9.1 | -7.5 |
| Difference | | | -2.1 | -3.7 | -0.3 |

Source: Y-9C call reports and CRSP.

### Figure 12. Total CRE with growth conditioned on construction

| C&D cohort | CRE cohort | Number of BHCs | Average change in MCR (percent) | 95 percent confidence bounds (percent) | |
|---|---|---|---|---|---|
| | | | | Lower | Upper |
| Under 100 percent | Over 300 percent and > 50 percent growth | 6 | -11.9 | -15.8 | -8.0 |
| Under 100 percent | Under 300 percent or < 50 percent growth | 140 | -8.6 | -9.3 | -7.8 |
| Difference | | | -3.3 | -7.2 | -0.6 |

Source: Y-9C call reports and CRSP.

added decline in MCR is no longer statistically significant. This lack of significance may be due at least in part to small sample size, because only six BHCs had a CLD ratio lower than 100 percent while simultaneously exceeding the total CRE 300 percent concentration level and meeting the 36-month CRE growth component.

# Part 6: Conclusion

This paper reviews bank failures during the recent economic downturn in the context of the 2006 inter-agency guidance. Three findings emerge from our analysis that provide a valuable perspective on the guidance. First, many banks identified as having high levels of CRE concentration levels either failed or saw their market valuations decline. Second, banks that lowered their CRE concentration levels did so primarily by reducing their exposures to CLD loans. Finally, we observed banks that were identified as having high CRE concentration levels actually expanding their CRE portfolios, primarily by increasing their holdings of non-CLD CRE loans.

We have discussed how the language of the guidance clearly states that the supervisory criteria were not intended to set hard caps on banking institutions' CRE concentration levels, but rather to define a level above which banks should be able to demonstrate enhanced credit risk management, which may include stress tests of the appropriate level of sophistication. We have found that, while the number of banks for which the supervisory criteria are applicable has declined dramatically since 2007, the criteria are still applicable for a non-trivial share of banks that holds a disproportionate amount of CRE loans. Further, we have found that the growth component, an oft-overlooked component of the total ratio criteria, significantly limits the number of institutions for which the criteria applies.

We have also validated the concerns that motivated the issuance of the guidance: CRE concentrations indeed have been a significant factor in post-2006 bank failures. Concentrated exposure to CLD loans, in particular, appears to have been the dominant risk driver. Further, we have found that banks have responded to market conditions and the supervisory criteria by shrinking their holdings of CRE portfolios, particularly with respect to their CLD loan portfolios. Finally, we have demonstrated that regulators' concerns regarding CRE concentrations are also evident in market-based measures of bank condition: Banks with excessive CRE concentrations saw greater declines in market capital ratios during the recent economic downturn.

# Appendix

The 2006 interagency guidance regarding CRE lending did not establish specific CRE lending limits or caps; rather, the guidance set forth supervisory criteria to serve as levels of bank CRE concentration above which they may be identified for further supervisory analysis. According to the guidance, institutions could be subject to further analysis if their

1.  loans for construction, land, and land development (CLD) represent 100 percent or more of the institution's total risk-based capital, or

2.  total non-owner-occupied CRE loans (including CLD loans), as defined, represent 300 percent or more of the institution's total risk-based capital, and further, that the institution's non-owner-

occupied CRE loan portfolio has increased by 50 percent or more during the previous 36 months

Owner-occupied CRE loans were not broken out by financial institutions in call report data until 2007; therefore, it was not possible to accurately measure the three-year growth rate of a bank's non-owner-occupied CRE portfolio—and correctly apply the growth component—until late in 2010. Given this data limitation, the historical analysis in this report often uses a measure of the second criteria without this condition applied. This appendix illustrates the correct calculations using the post-2007 call report definitions.

## Figure 13. Calculation of supervisory criteria with post-2007 call report data

**Construction concentration criterion: Ratio of CLD loans to total risk-based capital > 100 percent**

| Column (#) | Call report item | Item (#) | FFIEC 031 | FFIEC 041 |
|---|---|---|---|---|
| (C1) | 1–4 family residential construction loans | RC-C 1a(1) | RCONF158 | RCONF158 |
| (C2) | Other construction loans and all land development loans and other land loans | RC-C 1a(2) | RCONF159 | RCONF159 |
| (R1) | Total risk-based capital | RC-R 21 | RCFD3792 | RCFD3792 |

**Criterion: (C1 + C2) / (R1) > 1**

**Total CRE concentration criterion: Ratio of total non-owner-occupied CRE loans to total risk-based capital > 300 percent**

| Column (#) | Call report item | Item (#) | FFIEC 031 | FFIEC 041 |
|---|---|---|---|---|
| (C3) | Loans securitized by multi-family properties | RC-C 1d | RCON1460 | RCONF1460 |
| (C4) | Loans secured by other non-farm, non-residential properties (non-owner-occupied) | RC-C 1e(2) | RCONF161 | RCONF161 |
| (C5) | Loans to finance CRE | RC-C M-3 | RCFD2746 | RCFD2746 |

**Criterion: Ratio of total non-owner-occupied CRE loans to total risk-based capital > 300 percent and growth in non-owner-occupied CRE portfolio over the previous 36 months > 50 percent**

(C1 + C2 + C3 + C4 + C5) / (R1) > 3 and
(C1 + C2 + C3 + C4 + C5) [current quarter] / (C1 + C2 + C3 + C4 + C5) [12 quarters ago] > 1.5

Source: 2006 interagency guidance and call reports.